COMMUNITY CONNECTIONS
?

HOW DO WE LIVE TOGETHER?
MOUNTAIN LIONS

BY LUCIA RAATMA

CHERRY LAKE
Publishing

Published in the United States of America by Cherry Lake Publishing
Ann Arbor, Michigan
www.cherrylakepublishing.com

Content Adviser: Stephen S. Ditchkoff, PhD, Associate Professor, School of Forestry and
Wildlife Sciences, Auburn University
Reading Adviser: Cecilia Minden-Cupp, PhD, Literacy Consultant

Photo Credits: Cover and page 1, ©Helen E Grose, used under license from Shutterstock, Inc.;
page 5, ©Phillip Holland, used under license from Shutterstock, Inc.; page 7, ©Melanie DeFazio,
used under license from Shutterstock, Inc.; page 9, ©Patrick Hermans, used under license from
Shutterstock, Inc.; page 11, ©Dennis Donohue, used under license from Shutterstock, Inc.;
page 13, ©Joshua Haviv, used under license from Shutterstock, Inc.; page 15, ©iStockphoto.com/
harrysimpsonphotography; page 17, ©iStockphoto.com/JohnPitcher; page 19, ©iStockphoto.com/
banjoboy02; page 21, ©Geoffrey Kuchera, used under license from Shutterstock, Inc.

LIBRARY OF CONGRESS CATALOGING-IN-PUBLICATION DATA
Raatma, Lucia.
  How do we live together? Mountain lions / by Lucia Raatma.
    p. cm.—(Community connections)
  Includes bibliographical references and index.
  ISBN-13: 978-1-60279-625-6
  ISBN-10: 1-60279-625-4
  1. Puma—Juvenile literature. 2. Human-animal relationships—Juvenile
literature. I. Title. II. Title: Mountain lions.
  QL737.C23R235 2010
  599.75'24—dc22   2009027885

Cherry Lake Publishing would like to acknowledge the
work of The Partnership for 21st Century Skills. Please
visit www.21stcenturyskills.org for more information.

Printed in the United States of America
Corporate Graphics Inc.
January 2010
CLSP06

MOUNTAIN LIONS

CONTENTS

HOW DO WE LIVE TOGETHER?

WHAT'S OUTSIDE?

"Woof!" Your dog is barking. He looks out the window into the backyard. You look out, too. A large animal moves in the shadows. Neighbors have spotted mountain lions lately. Is there one outside?

Have you ever seen a mountain lion in your yard?

Mountain lions sometimes wander into backyards. They might just be passing by. Maybe they are looking for food. They also go to farms. Farmers get angry when mountain lions attack cows and sheep. Everyone worries about the safety of children and pets.

Mountain lions can be very dangerous animals.

Most people are afraid of mountain lions. But many neighborhoods were built in mountain lion **habitats**. The animals still need food and shelter. Let's take time to learn more about mountain lions.

There is not enough natural space for mountain lions.

Take a look around your neighborhood. Is land being cleared to build more houses or roads? What animals live in the green areas being cleared away?

A CLOSER LOOK AT MOUNTAIN LIONS

Mountain lions are **mammals**. Sometimes they are called **cougars** or **pumas**. They are also known as **catamounts** or **panthers**. These big cats weigh between 100 and 200 pounds (45 and 91 kilograms). They have large paws and strong legs.

Mountain lions can run fast and jump high to catch other animals.

Mountain lions used to live in many states. People often hunted them. These animals are almost gone from the eastern states. The Florida panther is now **endangered**. Today, mountain lions are most common in the western states. Some live in Canada and South America.

Mountain lions are very rare in some parts of the United States.

Mountain lions are **predators**. They eat other animals, such as deer and elk. They also eat rabbits and bighorn sheep. Mountain lions usually stay away from people. But they will attack humans in some cases. They also attack pets and farm animals if they are hungry. How can we get along with these predators?

Mountain lions need plenty of fresh meat to survive.

Can you guess how mountain lions help humans? One way is by hunting **prey**, such as deer. This keeps deer numbers down. Too many deer in an area can cause problems. Can you think of some other ways mountain lions can be helpful?

SHARING OUTDOOR SPACES

Mountain lions are powerful. Seeing them can scare people. Some people think that mountain lions should be hunted again. Others think the big cats have a right to find food. There are ways to respect these wild animals and still stay safe.

It is easy to see why people are scared of mountain lions!

If you go hiking, always go in a group. A mountain lion is more likely to attack a person who is alone. If you see a mountain lion, don't run away. Make lots of noise! Look as big and fierce as you can. The mountain lion will probably run off.

It is best to avoid mountain lions if you can.

DANGER!

HIGH MOUNTAIN
LION ACTIVITY

ENTER AT YOUR OWN RISK

There are ways to keep your pets safe, too. Let them sleep inside at night. Always feed them inside, too. Pet food can attract animals that mountain lions like to hunt. Farm animals should be kept behind tall fences. It is important for us to share the great outdoors!

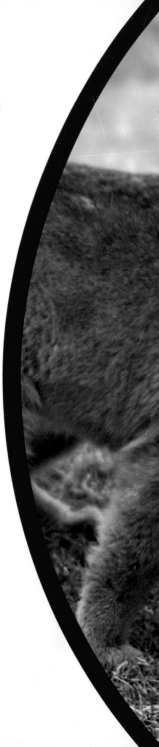

Mountain lions deserve our respect.

Mountain lions are beautiful creatures. Do you want to know more about them? Ask questions the next time you visit the zoo. Or talk to experts from the local wildlife department. They will be happy to share information with you.

GLOSSARY

catamounts (CAT-uh-mounts) another name for mountain lions

cougars (KOO-gurz) another name for mountain lions

endangered (en-DAYN-jurd) at risk of dying out

habitats (HAB-uh-tats) the places and natural conditions in which plants and animals live

mammals (MAM-uhlz) warm-blooded animals that are usually covered in hair, have backbones, give birth to live young, and make milk to feed their babies

panthers (PAN-thurz) another name for mountain lions

pumas (POO-muhs) another name for mountain lions

predators (PRED-uh-turz) animals that hunt and eat other animals

prey (PRAY) animals that are hunted and eaten by predators

FIND OUT MORE

BOOKS

Caper, William. *Florida Panthers: Struggle for Survival*. New York: Bearport Publishing, 2008.

Macken, JoAnn Early. *Cougars*. Pleasantville, NY: Gareth Stevens Publishing, 2009.

WEB SITES

BioKIDS Critter Catalog: Mountain Lion, Puma, Cougar

www.biokids.umich.edu/critters/Puma_concolor/
Learn more about mountain lions, and see pictures of them in the wild.

National Geographic: Mountain Lion

animals.nationalgeographic.com/animals/mammals/mountain-lion.html
Read about mountain lions and how they live.

San Diego Zoo Animal Bytes—Mammals: Mountain Lion

www.sandiegozoo.org/animalbytes/t-puma.html
Find out more about mountain lions and how people have learned to live with them.

INDEX

24

ABOUT THE AUTHOR

Lucia Raatma has written dozens of books for young readers. She and her family live in the Tampa Bay area of Florida. They enjoy visiting a Florida panther named Lucy at the local zoo.